CHILD KIDNAPPING UK ROSTER

UK Immigration file: Man 99-785

Excerpts from "To Steal a Child"

Aftermaths of negligent, incompetent dismissive institutions

D.L. Baron

(Updated January 2020)

Child Kidnapping UK Roster
Copyright © 2019 by D.L. Baron

All rights reserved. No part of this publication may be reproduced, distributed, or transmitted in any form or by any means, including photocopying, recording, or other electronic or mechanical methods, without the prior written permission of the author, except in the case of brief quotations embodied in critical reviews and certain other non-commercial uses permitted by copyright law.

Tellwell Talent
www.tellwell.ca

ISBN
978-0-22882-227-1 (Paperback)
978-0-22882-228-8 (eBook)

Table of Contents

Introduction 1
Foreword 2
Overview 3
Brief History 5
Home Office "Statement of Purpose and Aims" 8
Responsibilities of the Immigration and
    Nationality Directorate 9
The Criminal Justice System 9
Bureaucratic Roster 10
Conclusion 13
Epilogue-1 14
Epilogue-2 17
Excerpt US Law & Justice: February 1, 2018. 20

Sunday Times – July 6, 2003.

www.endchildexploitation.org.uk

A British newspaper article from The Sunday Times was titled "Secret Courts That Steal Our Children". Published on July 6-03, it exposed a litany of complaints against the Family Courts of England and Wales including - the Family Division of the High Court before which Patricia's case had been heard.

The article cast doubt on the credibility of witnesses used in Family Court. It questioned the evaluation of evidence on "balance of probability" rather than "beyond reasonable doubt" - a higher standard of proof obligatory to other courts. Criticism was leveled at Family Court's "culture of secrecy that shielded flawed deductions from public scrutiny". Statistics of holding accountable those who made false allegations, committed perjury or abused the system, showed that not only did the UK justice system fail to exercise responsibility in these areas, it also demonstrated disinterest in doing so.

INTRODUCTION

Clearly, the British criminal justice system had a double standard in prosecuting crime.

Moreover, it offered an explanation for UK authorities' dismissive attitude when confronted with their negligent handling of Patricia's kidnapping.

Technically - when it can be shown that a judge has made a mistake, there should exist a mechanism for appeal. In this case, with overwhelming evidence showing a miscarriage of justice, neither UK authorities, their courts, nor their judicial regulating bodies would take corrective action - substantiating our accusations that UK authorities were complicit in child kidnapping.

Since publishing this manuscript in 2018, statistics have shown this problem is only getting worse.

Foreword

On February 7th, 1999, a phone call from Canada to Ysgol Friars School in North Wales - inquiring about irregularities surrounding Patricia's school registration was never returned. In a second call the next day, neither Secretary Ann Jones nor the Principal - Neil Foden, followed up. Had they done so at that time, had they called the police to investigate, the damaging consequences that followed could not have happened. This deliberate negligence would be regarded as accessory to child kidnapping.

On behalf of Patricia, her family and many other victims, shedding light on the British Government's violations of basic principles of justice, set the stage to make these events public.

Thorough documentation is in the original manuscript *"To Steal a Child"* published in 2015 and available on Amazon Kindle.

Overview

The purpose in documenting this story was to show how society functions on trust and how easily that trust is betrayed and – how a criminal investigation can go wrong.

As case histories demonstrate, the first sign of a problem is when evidence is being ignored. Usually traced to an officious bureaucrat, reluctance to change the direction of an investigation is fraught with consequences. Short sightedness coupled with a refusal to admit a mistake can lead to a selective interpretation of the facts. In such an environment, investigations quickly become tainted. They travel along incomprehensible paths until errant facts become a brick wall. When fresh insight is most needed, people shift blame, plead ignorance, try to hide offending facts, and a miscarriage of justice is well on the way. Politics, expediency and misplaced deference to colleague solidarity add to the problem.

On the international front, it was shown how UK authorities treated Zambian institutions as irrelevant jurisdictions. They did nothing to assist the Zambian Foreign Office to carry out their role as monitor and protector of the welfare of its citizens abroad. Not once did the Home Office initiate or facilitate the involvement of Zambian officials to resolve this international incident, and not once was Patricia's family in Zambia contacted. No effort was made to enhance the family relationship. What was done, destroyed it.

The brutal rape of my daughter's mind was not sanctioned by an outcast third world dictatorship that isolates families as government policy, but by a country with a long legal history supported by democratic institutions. By attacking the integrity of the family, this reversal of roles had the predictable result.

In dealing with treachery, naïveté on this level is inexcusable. Is it any wonder there is a mistrust of the system? One would have expected better.

My family was first victimized by kidnappers. When cover-up became more important than professionalism and upholding the law, we were victimized a second time – by bureaucrats paid to deal with this problem.

Brief History

In June 1998, after initiating a meeting with Chief Kalindawalo and the family in Zambia, everyone agreed thirteen year old Patricia would be sent to join her family in Canada.

On August 22nd, Patricia was illegally removed from her Zambian jurisdiction by William Hall - a British citizen. A complete stranger to the family, he was the unmarried father to the female kidnapper's fourth child. The female accomplice was Innocentia Lewis (Chirwa). A single mother with four children from three fathers, she was known to the family.

Documentary evidence would eventually show a premeditated plan to use Patricia as cheap labour in the care of Mrs. Lewis' four children - the youngest being six months.

Unknown to Patricia's family at the time, conclusive evidence eventually surfaced that UK Immigration had issued a fraudulent visa; that Patricia was registered in school illegally; that she had been placed under a Deportation Order back to Zambia and – that UK Immigration was covering up their complicity in a child kidnapping case by withholding evidence.

With negligent, incompetent and dismissive agencies now taking over her case, the ensuing severe psychological pressure, browbeating and intimidation led to Patricia's total alienation from her family. Prior to all contact being cut, her calls to Canada from a phone booth threatening to kill herself were treated by UK police as crank calls not to be believed.

The criminality which began in Zambia continued in the UK. While Patricia was still a minor, the kidnappers threw her out of the house. She eventually got pregnant and became a single mother – all without her family's knowledge and still the responsibility of UK agencies.

Early on, Mrs. Lewis tried extorting money from the family. She claimed a false family relationship, lied repeatedly to authorities, and perjured herself in court proceedings.

When Patricia was maliciously manipulated to accuse her father of sexual abuse, three police investigations proved these allegations to be false, including Patricia's admission as documented in "To Steal a Child". Ignored by the authorities over the years, was Mrs. Lewis' history of making false criminal allegations as a means to get her way.

Parallel to this degenerate treatment of my family, there was a two year hiatus in family court. After a dozen hearings, it was established this court did not have jurisdiction; that the solicitors had misrepresented the parents' marital status – fundamental to the direction of the case; and – that the judge had ended the court case two weeks before evidence arrived – evidence the judge himself had asked for – that would have justified a criminal prosecution for child kidnapping.

In strikingly antiquated, colonial arrogance, all legal documentation, evidence, affidavits, etc. from Zambia were routinely dismissed by UK authorities as irrelevant. So much for UK's (dis)respect for the Zambian justice system.

Numerous independent British investigations have shown how UK's legal system leads to disrepute – particularly when dealing with child abduction.

HOME OFFICE "STATEMENT OF PURPOSE AND AIMS"

From: www.homeoffice.gov.uk

- To work with individuals and communities to build a safe and just society.
- To deliver policies and responsibilities fairly, effectively and efficiently.
- To reduce international crime in cooperation with the international community, including - trafficking in people.
- To ensure effective delivery of justice by avoiding unnecessary delay and through efficient investigation, detection, prosecution and court procedures.
- To engage with and support the victim and support families.
- To regulate entry to the United Kingdom effectively. To provide fair, fast and effective programs for dealing with visitors.

Responsibilities of the Immigration and Nationality Directorate

- To deter and detect people who break immigration rules.
- To work closely with immigration authorities in other countries.
- To regulate entry into the UK effectively.

The Criminal Justice System

- To provide a service in which the public can have confidence. ???

BUREAUCRATIC ROSTER

Included is a list of the individuals and agencies responsible for this bureaucratic farce, waste of public resources and destruction of the family.

A – Neil Foden – **Ysgol Friars School** Principal, Bangor, North Wales, No reply – No inquiry – Illegal school registration – No assistance – "get a lawyer".

B – Mrs. Gill Luther-Jones – **Ministry of Education and Social Services** – Dismissive – No assistance – "get a solicitor".

C – Sgt. Allison Cooke, **Colwyn Bay Police** – Incomplete investigation – ignored perjury.

D – **Chief Inspector** J. I. Jones, Chief Constable M. Argent, Alan Dylan, Special Branch, Sgt. Barry Edwards, Inspector P. Gaffey – Negligence – Incompetence – refused to act on section 1207 – child kidnapping.

E – Dr. H. Edwards, **Headmaster College Menai** – no reply – kept school records confidential.

F – Barry Thomas, **College Menai** – refused assistance – quoted confidentiality.

G – Nicola Ware – **British High Commission** – Lusaka – "get a solicitor" refrain.

H – Andrew Cullens – UK Immigration / **Home Office** – covered up fraudulent visa.

I – Mark Clough – **UK Immigration** – covered up fraudulent visa – no assistance.

J – Frank Ardley – **Home Office** – "too busy".

K – Peter Wint – Paula Widdison – **Jackson & Canter Solicitors** – incompetence – sabotaged court hearings – misrepresented fundamentals.

L – **Judges** Parry, Hughes, Hedley, Sumner – ignored evidence, pawns in a misguided case.

M – Mr. M. Hinchliffe – **Director of Legal Services** – pawn in a misguided case.

N – Jack Straw – **Minister of Immigration** – ultimate jurisdiction – no replies.

O – **Lusaka High Commission** / Home Office – negligence and cover up.

P – **CAFCASS** Barbara Norris – incomplete investigation report – ignored legal documentation from Zambia.

Q – Mr. D. Fabby, **Legal Services Commission** caseworker – legal aid irregularities fiasco.

R – Jane M. Betts, Shirley Burgess, A. Leeman – **Office for the Supervision of Solicitors** – arbitrary timelines – no resolution.

S – H. Stella Ramiah, **Legal Services Ombudsman**, Manchester – no assistance.

T – **Judicial Review** requests routinely ignored.

Conclusion

Contrary to their Oaths of Office and despite the training, this case is a clear example of negligent, incompetent and hypocritical practices of some UK bureaucrats.

The legacies of injustice no doubt explain many of the terrorist repercussions endemic in the UK today.

In sharp contrast to the United Kingdom, the Government of the United States has acted on child abduction and trafficking with a proclamation UK legislators need to emulate.

Until then, the criminality in the UK will continue to grow.

Epilogue-1

January 28, 2016

After many years of no communication, on Sunday, March 1st, 2015 - sixteen years and seven months after having been illegally taken from her family, I received an unexpected phone call from Patricia from somewhere in the UK. She was now thirty years old. Asking what had happened to her, she said she had married, divorced and had a four year old daughter.

Her tone had a mocking and accusatory manner over unresolved issues clearly brought on by her ordeal. She did not come across as genuine - probably no surprise, considering her history - and seemed to be pushed to make this call. Dealing with her twisted stay in the UK would have to come after she has a chance to read this book. She gave me her phone number which I gave to her sister. Apparently they are now on Facebook.

I am not a psychologist but – since receipt of the May 29-02 court transcript, Patricia seemed to have developed a split personality in order to cope emotionally. She seems to routinely side tract issues relating to her kidnapping and removal from Zambia. The way things usually go, sooner or later she would have to deal with the truth.

Since arriving in the UK, Patricia's family received only disturbing news from agencies involved in her case. Her call - with its semi-confident tone, gave me the green light to finish this story.

Early on a young life needlessly suffered brutal exploitation and psychological damage. There was never a kind or sympathetic note to bring the family together from anyone. Her family's efforts on her behalf are now documented in this text. What remains to be seen is her on-going ability to deal with the failures of the system that cost her her family. That she survived her ordeal this far, is a miracle.

Back on February 8th, 1999, I had phoned Ysgol Friars School to inquire about irregularities surrounding Patricia's registration. Neither Secretary Ann Jones nor the school Principal - Neil Foden, replied. Had they done so at that time, had they requested a proper investigation, most of the damaging and expensive consequences that followed - could not have happened. In most jurisdictions, this negligence would be regarded as accessory to child kidnapping.

On behalf of Patricia, her family and many other victims, shedding light on the British Government's violation of a basic principle of justice - **the laws of the land cannot be used to defend an illegal act** - set the stage for making these events public.

February 2018

Twenty years later, school records, court records, immigration and police records were routinely kept secret in a massive cover-up to protect those responsible for this miscarriage of justice. All the while, Patricia's whereabouts, communication and circumstances have been kept secret or sabotaged with perjury not held to account.

Meanwhile, the kidnappers continue their intimidation in a sustained effort to avoid a criminal prosecution. In a last short phone call a year ago, Patricia was in tears over her inability to deal with her circumstances. With no statute of limitations on child kidnapping, her family persists in this unresolved criminal matter.

Dedicated to the many victims of international child abduction, making these events public is intended to hold UK agencies and the perpetrators accountable with – a warning to other families who may end up in similar circumstances.

D. Baron, Canada

Epilogue-2

August 2nd, 2019

The twenty-first year of Patricia's kidnapping, she arrived in Vancouver with her seven year old daughter on a visit arranged by her sister. They returned three weeks later with mixed success as her split personality was even more evident. I sum up her visit for the family.

August 25, 2019

From day one I observed that Patricia had deep-seated anger and hostility issues managing to hide her feelings as the occasion demands.

The first day she jumped out of my car with her daughter almost causing a police incident. The next day more anger and threatening to jump out of the car a second time. This was not normal behaviour.

A few hours of honest conversation about the truth would have explained a lot to her and allowed us to move on but she was determined not to listen.

She made false allegations about abandonment that were explained in the book - which clearly she had not read - nor understood due to her inadequate schooling. She repeatedly refused her sister's help over the negativity and psychological trauma she suffered. She refused to show us the Court Order that allowed her daughter to visit Canada.

The hope is the history will not damage Patricia's daughter despite the circumstances.

In the meantime we are preparing for court again. The expectation this time is these events will be look at properly.

August 27th, 2019

Patricia and her daughter returned to the UK with none of her issues resolved.

October 7, 2019

Affectionally known as Mazulu, Fatness Zulu passed away on October 7, 2019 in Petauke, Zambia. Patricia's mother was one week short of her 62nd birthday. At least left behind now, is the hatred and suffering that made her life so needlessly difficult.

December 30, 2019 Re:
Last Will and Testament

Hello Patricia - At some point you will have to face the history of your early life. For 21 years you have been relentlessly turned against your family. We have been very patient hoping you would break free of the lies and misinformation you continue to be subjected to. William laying his problems on you is just another example of his refusal to deal with problems he and Inno created.

At 34 years of age, you should have enough experience to understand the truth. Unfortunately, your brainwashing is clearly evident in your refusal to hear any explanations at all. I feel you are too weak to prevent your kidnappers from stealing your inheritance.

For this reason, I had no choice but to have my solicitors remove you and Naimah from my Will.

Take care, Love, Dad

Excerpt US Law & Justice: February 1, 2018.

President Donald J. Trump Proclaims January 2018 as National Slavery and Human Trafficking Prevention Month

During National Slavery and Human Trafficking Prevention Month, we recommit ourselves to eradicating the evils of enslavement that have no place in our world. We pledge to do all in our power to end the horrific practice of human trafficking plaguing innocent victims around the world.

Millions of people are currently victims of human trafficking for both sex and labor. Traffickers prey on victims by promising a life of hope and greater opportunity. Through violence and intimidation, they deliver only enslavement and work in brothels, factories, private homes and countless industries.

The US Department of State has contributed millions to the Global Fund to End Modern Slavery due to the critical need for cross-nation collaborative action to counter human trafficking. The President signed an Executive Order to dismantle transnational criminal organizations, assist survivors of human trafficking, eradicate forced labor from global supply chains and improve efforts to recognize, prevent and report on human trafficking.

The United States will forever be a place that values and protects human life and dignity. Let us redouble efforts to ensure that modern day slavery comes to a long overdue end.

NOW, THEREFORE, I, DONALD J. TRUMP, President of the United States of America, by virtue of the authority vested in me by the Constitution and the laws of the United States, do hereby proclaim January 2018 as National Slavery and Human Trafficking Prevention Month, culminating in the annual celebration of National Freedom Day on February 1, 2018.

I call upon industry associations, law enforcement, private businesses, faith-based and other organizations of civil society, schools, families, and all Americans to recognize our vital roles in ending all forms of modern slavery and to observe this month with appropriate programs and activities aimed at ending and preventing all forms of human trafficking.

IN WITNESS WHEREOF, I have hereunto set my hand this twenty-ninth day of December, in the year of our Lord two thousand seventeen.

Donal J. Trump

www.ingramcontent.com/pod-product-compliance
Lightning Source LLC
LaVergne TN
LVHW011901060526
838200LV00054B/4469